To Julia and Emory,

With best wishes for God's richest blessings now and always,

Al Hall

December 28, 1997

It's Trimmed in White
If Color Makes Any Difference to You

Al Hall

Baltimore, Maryland

It's Trimmed in White If Color Makes Any Difference to You

Copyright © 1997 Al Hall

All rights reserved under International and Pan-American copyright conventions. No part of this book may be reproduced, stored in a retrieval system, or transmitted in any form, electronic, mechanical, or other means, now known or hereafter invented, without written permission of the publisher. Address all inquiries to the publisher.

Library of Congress
Cataloging in Publication Data
ISBN 1-56167-363-3

Library of Congress Card Catalog Number:
97-067147

Published by

8019 Belair Road, Suite 10
Baltimore, Maryland 21236

Manufactured in the United States of America

*Dedicated to
"the Bride of Christ,"
the church.*

This book of poems so accurately captures the "little things" that count but most often are taken for granted or ignored—caring, giving, selflessness. It recalls a simple life in the African American experience; it is the gospel in plain talk that all can understand and embrace—spiritual.

—Lavatus V. Powell
Vice President of a Fortune 100 Company and
Elder of the Presbyterian Church, Cincinnati, Ohio

As a special friend of Al's for many years, his poetry for me is simple, yet profound, with a tremendous impact because of its revealing of truth. Everyone can find something in common with his writing.

—Gary Moore
Alexandria, Virginia

This collection is an eye-opener to realism which causes the reader to reflect on life. Al expresses strong commitment and tender emotions in poems that depict images of the past and present, with a glimpse of the future. This book truly warms the heart.

—Lottie Blalock Hall, Former Diaconate Chair
Braddock Church, Alexandria, Virginia

The author is able to express his thoughts, feelings, and observations—which others have also felt—in clear, concise, and rhythmic poetry. The messages he shares are for all of us, whether man or woman, young or old, rich or poor. He has a true understanding of the anguish each of us periodically feels, and shares his thoughts in a straightforward manner.

—Jerald N. Hutchins, Missions Chair
First United Methodist Church, Vancouver, Washington

Foreword

Al Hall has been writing poems for much of his life. In the fifteen years that we have worked together, he has produced countless poems as his gifts to colleagues—retirees, returnees, those departing for other jobs, getting married, or celebrating special occasions. Al's poems are on their walls or in their scrapbooks. These are private poems, handcrafted, made to order, suited to the recipient, and read aloud a single time.

Al also has written public poems, commissioned for delivery at various ceremonies, sad or glad, with ample notice or at the last moment. These too have been specific, tailored, fitting.

Here are published poems, his second collection, available to all. Most deal with church, religion, God. All deal with self and with others, a hallmark of Al Hall.

You will find Al's words, rhymes, and revelations simple or subtle, plain or profound, amusing or shocking, always insightful, grounded in goodness, centered in God's love.

Al's poems, like any poems, are made to be read aloud. Read these poems aloud. Read them with your family, read them to friends, read them at a meeting or in your place of worship. Listen for Al's voice, listen for God's voice, as you add your own inflections.

Brian Payne, Ph.D.
Deacon, Little River United Church of Christ
Annandale, Virginia

Contents

Meeting Needs 1
When the Pastor Is Away 2
Who Will Be There for the Pastor? 3
Good-bye to Loneliness 5
Take Time to Share 7
Silent Screaming 8

Servanthood and Commitment 11
Wrong Way 12
I'll Be a Bird for Christ 13
Lord, Help Me Around This Curve 15

Self Reflections 17
Eating with Pigs 18
Limited Expression 20
A Hesitant Confession 22
Where to Turn 23
Wherein Lies the Trouble 25

Prayer and Faith 27
Come Quickly and Deliver Me 28
Baptismal Joy at Christmas 30
My Psalm 31
Cross Over to the Other Side 32
My Red Sea Experience 34

Empty My Cup   36
A New Conductor   37
Message from the Nonbelievers   39
Powerline   40
A Prayer   41

Seeing People As They Are   43
Whose Lows—Yours or Mine?   44
Held Hostage in Her House   46
Being a Pastor   47
Eat Until the Starving Are Fed   50
See Me for Who I Am   52
Label Him Man   53
It's Trimmed in White If Color Makes Any Difference to You   55

Forgiveness   57
Suffer the Consequences   58
My Savior   59
Locked in the Past   60
I Want to Ask His Forgiveness   61
Pocketful of Forgiveness   62
His Cup Runneth Over with Revenge   63

Set Apart   65
Falling in Line with the World   66

No Reflection on You   67
Uniqueness   68
Be a Part of the Worship Service   70
Sometimes   72
A Slave to Sin No More   74
Make Him Turn and Run   75
Satan, I'm Going to Tell Jesus on You   77
Peculiar People   78

Death   79
Believe on Him   80
Fifty Years from Now   81
Preparing for the Inevitable   82
When Life Is Closing In   83
We've Been Forgotten Day   84

Humor   85
Church Member Goes on Vacation   86
Blame the Pastor   87
Surprise! Surprise! Surprise!   90
Pointing Fingers at Them   93
The Pastor's Wife   95
Invitations to Weddings and Funerals   97
You're Sitting in My Seat   99
Get Me from the Church on Time   100

Meeting Needs

When the Pastor Is Away

Maybe the pastor wants some time alone,
To reflect on what is on his mind.
But we can't leave him out there by himself.
He would never leave us behind.

Now and then he visits his relatives,
Whom he may not have seen for a while.
He may spend time on the highway,
Being alone for every mile.

We do not have to show concern,
And then wait to see his good deeds.
We can show our love for what he has done,
And the way that he has met our needs.

We can show our love through moral support.
Spread love! Just let it abound!
We can keep on spreading it day by day.
There is plenty to go around.

Who Will Be There for the Pastor?

The pastor is always there when he is needed,
And he doesn't come because of pay.
He has a genuine interest in all the members,
And he shows it in a caring way.

He has been there for everybody else.
Now who is going to be there for him?
His members know that if he is needed,
He will still be there for them.

When babies are born, he is somewhere near.
He wants to share the wonderful joy.
He is right there with those smiling parents,
As they welcome each girl or boy.

He has stood by those going through divorce,
And by others whose parents have died.
He comforted one whose heart was breaking,
And another who just sat and cried.

He comes sometimes in the middle of the night.
He comes early during the day.
We are always glad to see him arrive,
Because he knows just what to say.

Quite often he feels at a loss for words,
But his presence fills such a need.
Whenever he speaks, there is so much love.
And there is a feeling of comfort, indeed.

Good-bye to Loneliness

There is no need for loneliness.
Someone needs to share
The thoughts they have inside them
With someone willing to care.

There are enough ears to listen
To all of one's little woes;
To the many, many worries
That keep one feeling low.

Seek out some other person;
There is someone who knows why.
There are other people just like you,
Who feel they're being passed by.

We don't need to feel so lonely,
Or keep our heads hung down.
To see the beauties of this world,
Look up and look around.

When have you made an effort
To do a kindly deed,
By looking out for someone else
Who also has a need?

If we stay too close to only self,
Then only self we can find.
We may get lost in the search,
Because we've been there all the time.

Search for what makes you happy;
Find it and let loneliness go.
There is a life of happiness
That all of us can know.

Take Time to Share

Everyone needs a time to share
With a spouse or with a friend;
The things that seem of most concern,
Reality—or things that might have been.

A time to share accomplishments,
Or talk about the day's defeats;
To discuss a burden or share a thought,
With the people whom we meet.

If you can find some time to share,
It's like breathing a real deep breath;
And when the sharing is over,
It's like tasting sweet success!

So share a thought with someone else.
Take time to talk a while.
The exchange of all the sorrows and joys
May be mixed with tears and smiles.

You can find time to do it,
And have some time to spare;
You can add hours to your very own day,
By taking the time to share!

Silent Screaming

Can you hear that silent screaming?
The sound is faint,
    yet audible,
    yet understandable,
    demanding a personal response.

The thoughts are not articulated.
But the feeling is communicated
    through facial expression,
    through action,
    through those wandering eyes.

Some real feelings may never be spoken,
But the silent screaming continues
    in the presence of family,
    in the presence of friends,
    and in the workplace.

Listen to that silent screaming!
Look around you and follow the sound.
    It's near.
    It's closer.
    It's here.

Sometimes it is within — yes, within.
    Silent screaming.
    Silent screaming.
    Silent screaming.

Servanthood and Commitment

Wrong Way

Take your vacation
    and fly away.
Are you getting ready
    for the judgment day?

You forget about the Lord
    when you're doing fine.
You might need Him
    at some other time.

Put others last
    and do for yourself.
There is no need to worry
    about anyone else.

Count all your riches
    as you store them up.
Never take part
    in the communion cup.

Glorify yourself
    when you sing your song
Oh, no, neighbor!
    This way is wrong!

I'll Be a Bird for Christ

There comes a time when we must speak.
There are times when we should not talk.
As deacons we must know the path,
That all of us should walk.

Church families need our care and love,
As we minister day by day.
We may not always know the words,
That God would have us say.

But we can ask Him to guide our tongue,
And make the words just come out right.
No matter whether we serve by day,
Or whether we serve at night.

We must minister to one another.
Our pastors need ministry, too.
Our spouses and families should be included.
This is something we must do.

We won't be able to do everything,
But we can do our very best.
We are servants who are now called deacons.
How can we do any less?

Some have reservations about serving as deacon.
They say this is for the birds.
If they could experience this act of servanthood,
They may change these piercing words.

I have no wings to fly away,
So I'm willing to pay the price.
If serving as deacon makes me a bird,
I'll be a bird for Christ!

Lord, Help Me Around This Curve

Lord, I can't stay on this winding road,
Unless you're here at the wheel.
I read your Word and talk with you,
And your Spirit is what I feel.

I'm willing to try as I have before.
I'll do my best to serve.
This road keeps winding and not going straight;
So help me around this curve.

You can drive and I will ride.
I know I can get a new start.
Serving you continues on this winding road,
But it begins within the heart.

Dear Lord, I wish you would straighten the road,
So that its beauty can be preserved.
I cannot travel it by myself;
I need you at every curve.

Yes, I'll remember you when it's going well.
I promise you that I will serve.
I need you at all points along the way,
But most desperately at every curve.

Self Reflections

Eating with Pigs

I may as well be eating dirt.
I could be eating twigs.
I'm about as low as I can go.
I'm eating with the pigs.

I asked for everything coming to me.
I wanted to take my share.
I left home and ran away.
I just was not happy there.

I found things out there to be real great.
I had a real splendid time.
I had a life that was mighty wild.
I found it so sublime.

Now my good times have all run out.
My friends have turned away.
Nobody knows that I exist,
Because I have no more money to pay.

Where is my father who let me go?
What is he doing right now?
He's taking care of all the servants.
I've got to find him somehow!

Yes, servants are living better than I,
And they are not eating twigs.
But I am as low as I've ever been;
I'm eating with the pigs.

Here I am, Father, take me in.
I know my actions were wrong.
Thank you for reaching out to me.
I'm glad to be back home.

Forgive me, Brother, for leaving you here;
I can see why you're so mad.
Things are rough in a fast-moving world;
So I'm returning to you and Dad.

Father, I thank you for this feast.
It's not like eating twigs.
It's a delicious meal and I'm so happy
To stop eating with the pigs.

Limited Expression

I can be with you in your sorrows.
I can share with you in your pain.
Somehow when you try to share with me,
It never is the same.

Self expression comes natural for me
When I need to comfort you.
But often when someone responds to me,
Expression is hard to do.

Don't mind my seeming ungrateful.
Forgive my seeming lack of concern.
I appreciate what everyone does for me;
With gratitude my heart still burns.

Even for the one who is closest to me,
Limited is my true expression.
I appreciate the warmth and kindness
Of all who hear this confession.

Sometimes I find myself speechless,
When I have so much to say.
I want to say thanks for all the joy
That comes to me each day.

If there is anything I can do for you,
I will help wherever I can.
If I'm not overjoyed when you do for me,
Please try to understand.

A Hesitant Confession

Why do shadows creep into life,
When the sun can shine right through?
What is it that makes us stumble,
And do the things we do?

How can we go for such a long while,
With the mountains we have to climb?
Why does it seem that they're just appearing,
When they've been there all the time?

Where is the place without all the sorrows
That come to us day after day?
Which way do we turn when we are tempted
To say the things we should not say?

Who is the person with none of these questions?
From where did he receive the light?
Let him lead others in the same direction,
To get on a path that's right.

If you're on the road that is leading you
To places you'd rather not go,
Now is the time to turn around.
Your direction is wrong—and you know!

Where to Turn

Who knows your life better than you?
Who sees inside your mind?
Do you expect your friends to solve
The problems they cannot find?

Don't look to others for peace of mind.
Try to work it out yourself.
If you need a friend to share your thoughts,
Then call somebody else.

If you understand what's wrong in your life,
Start working to make it right.
Or Satan will get the best of you;
He's always willing to fight.

God is there waiting to help you;
So let Him take command.
Be willing to let Him lead you.
Be ready to change your plans.

You may tell a friend just part of your story;
With God you can tell it all!
Hold up your weakening friends in prayer.
Don't let your brother fall!

The Bible tells how to be a Christian,
And how to have eternal life.
Do your best and when you need God,
He'll support you in your strife.

Wherein Lies the Trouble

There's always something brewing,
Trouble is simmering in the pot.
By the time the lid comes off,
The issue is piping hot.

There's war going on in another country,
But it's still too close to home.
It looks like there's trouble everywhere
That a person may choose to roam.

Bickering is present in the church.
It's one member after another.
Why can't this all be turned around,
So that one can help the other.

Families don't have the time to be family.
Somebody is always out.
They have things they need to share,
And they don't know what it's all about.

Friends can't build their relationships,
For they have no time to meet.
So they never experience the real true meaning
Of those talks that can be so sweet.

The neighborhood is a mighty fine place.
You couldn't appreciate living more.
And just when it appears that all is well,
There's trouble in the house next door.

Children grow up and go to school.
They are a blessing to the teacher's eye,
Until it's learned that the work is not done,
And your child didn't even try.

You've got two cars to make your runs.
At least, you will do your part.
But when it's time to pick the children up,
The cars won't even start.

Nothing around here is running smoothly.
I see trouble on every shore.
When I'm sure of a way to get rid of it,
There seems to be even more.

There must be some beginning point!
Where can this trouble be?
I could point my finger at everyone else,
But, first, I'll take a look at me.

Prayer and Faith

Come Quickly and Deliver Me

When they needed me I was there—
   in times of sorrow;
   in moments of suffering;
   in days of distress.

My heart was often heavy
   with the burden of their loss;
   with their hurt and uncontrollable pain;
   with the piercing arrow of their distress.

Their days of loneliness were my days of loneliness
   until I realized the joy of companionship;
   until I could have a visit with them;
   until we were able to comfort one another.

We served our God together
   through studying His Word;
   singing praises to His Holy Name;
   through prayer and fellowship.

Where did it all disappear?
  Where are those who care?
  Where are those who are concerned?
  Where are those who know my sorrow?

Where are all of the friendly faces?
  Reach out to me, somebody.
  Give me a helping hand.
  Is there anyone who understands?
  Why is this happening to me?

"Make haste, O God, to deliver me,"
  For I know that you are still near.
  I know that you will not leave me.
  I'm still depending on you.

Bless all of those who love you.
  Draw others closer to you.
  Forgive those who seek forgiveness.
  Forgive me as I forgive.

Baptismal Joy at Christmas

Praise God for His Son, Jesus.
Praise God for that wonderful birth.
Thank you, God, for giving us Christmas.
And for peace on this beautiful earth.

Thank you for the gift of eternal life,
As we are surrounded in a world of sin.
Thank you for making it possible
For all of us to enter within.

Thank you for those who are being baptized,
As we think of that cold, cold manger.
They are warm in the arms of Jesus.
He can keep them from harm and danger.

Lord, use them as an example
To help others recognize the worth
That comes with this holy ordinance;
The experience of this spiritual birth.

We rejoice with those who are being baptized,
On this special day in December.
May this Christmas Eve bring blessings
That they will always remember.

My Psalm

Dear Lord,

*Out of the depths of my heart
  I cry with praise and
  thanksgiving for the benefit
  of your showering love.*

*When I am lowest and feeling
  down and out, you are
  the One who takes me to
  unlimited happiness.*

*Whenever I don't know where
  to turn or what to do,
  I know that I can
  always depend on you.*

*Thank you for
  being my Father.
Make me more worthy of
  being your child.*

Amen.

Cross Over to the Other Side

Now is the time to cross the river,
*   while it is still narrow,*
*   while it's not raging with wild waters,*
*   and just a step will get you over*
*   to the other side.*

Don't wait too long to make your move,
*   to go in the right direction,*
*   to go toward a loving Savior,*
*   to move close to an Everlasting King*
*   who is waiting to take your hand.*

There is no need to wait any longer,
*   for the river is getting wider and wider*
*   as it flows to its destination;*
*   and the current is growing*
*   swifter and swifter;*
*   so you need to cross over now!*

You're getting closer to the ocean,
    and the river is surely deeper,
    and it's getting wider still!
    So don't stand there away from Jesus
    when you could cross over
    to the other side
    and be saved.

Do it now! Come on and cross over!
    Then let the waters run wild,
    into the ocean and far beyond!
    Your worries may not be ended,
    but you'll have someone to take them,
    and you'll be glad
    you trusted Him.

You'll be safe—on the other side.

My Red Sea Experience

Lord, part this Red Sea ahead of me,
For I'm at a total loss.
I've come all the way to this point in my life,
And now I just can't get across.

Please make a way for me to finish this task.
I'm being hindered on every side.
I know I can do it; I know I can!
But the Red Sea just had to rise.

I've faced a lot of Red Seas, Dear Lord,
But this time I need a change.
Is there some way to get me safely across?
Can anything be arranged?

This is my Red Sea experience, Lord;
It's my Red Sea special plea.
I'm depending on you to get me across.
Lord, open up this raging Red Sea!

I know what you did for Moses,
When he needed you to part the Red Sea.
And I have faith that if you did it for Moses,
You will do the same for me.

Lord, I don't need this Red Sea experience;
I surely don't need it today.
So please move this Red Sea away from me,
And help me to find my way.

I know my life will have some rain;
A lake or a river, there may be.
But why is it that I must face
The waves of this raging Red Sea?

Empty My Cup

Empty my cup, Lord,
    and fill it with your love.
Empty my mind of all the things
    that should not be there,
    and fill it with thoughts of you.

Help me to help others in
    their struggle to find peace
    of mind and heart.
Fill my cup with your love, Lord,
    and let me pour it where
    it is needed.

Help me to be willing to
    gather something new
    and share it in the
    name of love.

A New Conductor

Does your train keep jumping off the track,
Every time you turn a curve?
Could the devil be making an oil slick,
So that to him you'll turn and serve?

You'll have to watch him every mile,
Or he'll keep on wrecking your train.
He doesn't care if the sun's not shining,
For he works right through the rain.

Give your train problems to a new Conductor,
Who is powerful enough to keep His own.
Let God help you defeat the devil.
Don't try to make the journey alone!

With confidence you can travel then;
You can move on to your Heavenly Station.
Leave the devil there in his oily mess,
As you prepare for a celebration.

Don't regret leaving the devil behind;
Your train has no room for him.
But pick up the lost along the way;
You're commanded to reach out for them.

Then on the day of your arrival,
You'll be glad you did not turn back.
You'll be glad you found a new Conductor,
To keep your train on track.

Message from the Nonbelievers

He doesn't believe in Jesus Christ.
She doesn't believe in your God of love.
They don't need that for their existence;
They don't need those blessings from above.

He doesn't need to be religious.
It doesn't do a thing for him.
There may be a reason for seeking salvation,
But it's nothing that is clear to them.

They understand about science and politics,
And that is quite good enough.
So they don't need to waste their time
Listening to this Jesus stuff.

They're not looking to find salvation,
So don't try to present what's free.
They've got just about everything they need.
They are as content as they can be.

They're doing fine and they're very happy.
They don't even have a worry.
Perhaps they could speed things up a little,
But they see no need to hurry.

Powerline

He says he has no Power.
There seems to be a broken line.
He wonders what he's going to do.
His problem has now become mine.

I must help him make the connection.
Without Power, who runs his life?
He needs a Power beyond the kind
That is causing him so much strife.

For electrical power he can simply ask.
Someone will know what to do.
If he wants the Power that comes from above,
He'll have to ask for that, too.

Check your line to see if the Power
Flows freely everyday.
If you find your line making all connections,
Help someone else along the way.

A Prayer

Lord, I can be so very happy
Just sharing your Word with friends.
Please help me in all Your Power,
To reach away from sin.

Lord, help me to always respect my friends,
And realize their commitment to you.
Let me help them to be strong enough
To do what you want them to do.

I just want to be able, Lord,
To get through every day,
Without ever having to apologize
For saying what I should not say.

Lord, help me to read and understand
The message in your Holy Word.
Then help me to be willing to practice
The things I have already heard.

Lord, help me to stay in touch with you.
Help me leave temptation behind.
I want to search the scriptures
Until I find what I need to find.

Seeing People As They Are

Whose Lows—Yours or Mine?

I'd like to help when you're feeling low,
But I just don't have the time.
When I try to think about your lows,
I get real busy thinking about mine.

I go on smiling as if all is well,
And outwardly, things look just fine.
But I can't help you with your lows,
Because I'm too busy thinking about mine.

There've been times when I was way, way down.
I got in the valley and seemed to stay.
It appeared as if I'd never get out,
Although I took the time to pray.

You may not have noticed any of my lows.
Perhaps, you thought all was well.
Though not expressed in vivid words,
Those closest to me could tell.

At times your lows are more important.
We'll discuss my problems next time.
Whose lows shall we tackle today?
Will it be yours or mine?

Oh, we don't have to count the minutes;
And let's not measure the time.
Let's just pour our hearts out to one another,
With your concerns AND mine.

God is big enough to hear them all.
Just give Him a joyful try.
He can bring the lows right out of the valley,
And change each one to a high.

Held Hostage in Her House

There she was, a local hostage,
Being held on the second floor.
She had been captured right at home.
She hadn't even been out the door.

Her mother had suffered a serious illness,
And needed someone to take her in.
Perhaps she could have gone to a nursing home;
Maybe there's where she should have been.

But care by the children would be so much better,
She agreed to receive her mother.
She knew it would not be an easy task,
But thought the siblings would help each other.

Soon most of the care was left to her,
While others sometimes pitched in.
They would do a little and leave for home,
But she was right where she had always been.

If an aging parent wants to live with you,
Do what you feel in your heart,
But remember you cannot guarantee
That others will do their part.

Being a Pastor

*Being a pastor is a most rewarding occupation,
often filled with ups and downs,
successful moments and
moments of failure.*

*Being a pastor is a promising career,
to begin early
or late in life;
for the work involved
never ends, no matter
where one starts.*

*Being a pastor can keep one from
eating when hungry,
drinking when thirsty,
sleeping when exhausted, or
screaming when disgusted!*

*Being a pastor brings joy in knowing that
someone has been led to Christ,
that someone has been
spiritually lifted when ill, or
comforted during times of bereavement.*

Being a pastor often means being alone,
not going with the ways of the world,
and sometimes not supported by
those who are Christians.

Being a pastor qualifies one for long hours
on the telephone,
listening to the same
moaning and groaning,
and the complaining heard
so many times before.

Being a pastor brings one many smiles, compliments,
and invitations to special occasions
with families and friends
of the congregation.

Being a pastor certifies one for early information
about problems in the family,
the arrival of a new baby,
a forthcoming wedding or
a sudden death.

Being a pastor means being silent when
one would like to be speaking
and speaking when one would rather be quiet,
without having to worry about
the sins of omission or commission.

Being a pastor is not all joys and not all sorrows,
not receiving the award
for popularity or being gonged
for performances which are
not approved or well received
by the audiences.

Being a pastor is recognizing the call of God and,
like any other Christian,
making oneself available
to work for Him,
and follow His guidance
each day in every
word and deed.

Eat Until the Starving Are Fed

People elsewhere are starving;
So this food you cannot waste.
I cannot throw it all away;
So you must eat it up in haste.

Eat everything that's on your plate.
To waste food is such a shame.
That's why people keep on starving,
And you are part to blame.

Clean every bowl you see before you.
There is not enough left to save.
I know you can eat a little bit more;
Go ahead! Eat and be brave.

I often wonder whether this is the answer—
Cleaning every bowl because I'm able.
Am I eating to feed the starving world,
Or doing it to clear the table?

For years I've heard that I should eat it all,
Because some are starving and nearly dead.
I'm showing a pound for every ounce I eat,
And the starving are still not being fed.

Please don't do this to your children.
Try to help them understand.
Let them know that overeating
Can't help a starving land.

They can eat and eat, then eat some more.
They can clean their plates until they shine.
This will not help those who are starving,
But it can ruin one's peace of mind.

For after all the eating is done,
There comes the weight that is likely to follow.
And people elsewhere continue to starve;
Their stomachs continue to be hollow.

So put less food upon your plate.
Eat what you need and learn to give.
You do not have to clean the bowl
In order for others to live.

See Me for Who I Am

I'm only human
    and I hurt inside.
Do you not feel the pain?
I'm a person
    and I make mistakes.
Can you, in all of your perfection,
    tolerate even the least of these?
I'm a mortal man,
    so my sins will be noted.

Some day I'll be immortal,
    for my sins will be forgiven.
I'm a weak person
    but I have strong points, too.
I am an individual.
I am a separate being.
I am a man with vision.
I can see and respect you
    just as you are.
Can you see me?
Try!
Try!
Try!

Label Him Man

Label him man if he lives and breathes
  The same as other men do.
Don't write him off as an outcast,
  Because he doesn't look the same as you.

Label him man, for that he is;
  His heart is in the right place.
Don't discard what God has made;
  Don't slap him in the face.

Label him man with all his joys,
  But he has troubles, too.
Give him a chance to be himself;
  He should do the same for you.

Label him man without description,
  Such as disabled or white or black.
Don't let his appearance blind you;
  Don't let it hold you back.

Label him man with his possessions,
  And label him if he's broke.
Look for all the good in him,
  And not a subject for your next joke.

Label him man if he's a preacher,
  Or if he's just a real good friend.
He has feelings he wants to share;
  Why should he keep them in?

Label him man as chief executive,
  With concerns right to the top;
And even if he's not professional,
  Respect for him shouldn't stop.

Label him man from any race;
  Label him young or old.
Label him for what he is;
  Don't let him go undersold.

Label him man created by God,
  In the image of Himself.
If God has labeled His own creation,
  Who can label him anything else?

It's Trimmed in White If Color Makes Any Difference to You

So you want to know where I worship.
You need to have more facts.
You need information about the surroundings,
And some of the people my church attracts.

You're concerned about the songs we sing,
And about the kinds of prayers we pray.
You want to know what time the service ends,
Because you may decide to attend some day.

You're trying to find something that you're not asking.
I think I know where you're going with this.
I'll keep responding to the critical analysis,
So there will be nothing that I will miss.

My community speaks without saying a word.
It narrates its own composition.
You're welcome to be a part of the worship service.
We're not hung up on a person's position.

I have the feeling there are other questions.
What else do you need to know?
We worship Jesus, the Son of a living God,
And share His Word wherever we go.

Oh, you want to know if my church is White!
The real question has come to the light.
It should not matter what color it is,
Because one can worship in Black or White.

Let me tell you about my church.
I'll describe it since you want me to.
It's beautiful red brick, all trimmed in white,
If color makes any difference to you.

Forgiveness

Suffer the Consequences

When you sin you suffer the consequences,
Although God truly forgives.
But you have done somebody wrong,
And with yourself you have to live.

It makes no difference what you've done.
God can handle your biggest task.
He's ready to forgive your greatest sin.
All you have to do is ask.

Once the scar is made on your life,
In your mind it has taken its place.
God will forgive you for what you've done,
But it's something you've got to face.

After the sin has been committed,
You'll stop and see what you've done.
Seeing you've already gone too far,
You'll wish you could just up and run.

So run to God and get it right.
He's ready to hear your plea.
You don't have to suffer the rest of your life.
Forgiveness can set you free.

My Savior

I can sing about your
    forgiveness.
I can shout with joy
    and praise.
I know how it feels
    to be forgiven.
I'll serve you all
    my days.
Thank you for being a
    Savior,
Who watches over me.
Forgive me when I
    fail you.
And keep me close to thee.

Locked in the Past

Why can't you comfort your brother,
Disregarding the color of his skin?
Sometimes we get locked in the past,
Worrying about our neighbor's sins.

The past is a guide for the future,
But you must not blow your mind.
Don't worry about your evil neighbor,
Because God said, "Vengeance is mine."

Oh, sure someone has wronged you;
So you have someone to forgive.
It doesn't help to hold a grudge
When you can lighten your load and live.

We are often locked in the past, my friends,
While the present is ever so bright.
We waste time getting back at others,
Missing the warmth of the Heavenly Light.

Put behind you that desire for vengeance,
And grasp a hope that is sure to last.
Our God lives now and forever;
He is not all locked in the past.

I Want to Ask His Forgiveness

I love Daddy; don't let him die!
There is something I want to say.
I have not even spoken to him
Since that very awful day.

I told him how I hated his guts,
And hoped I would never see him again!
That is why he cannot die,
And leave me in all this pain.

Where is Daddy? Please tell me!
I have to see him now!
"Your dad has gone to another world,
But you will get along somehow."

"Here's a note he left for you.
It will make you feel good inside.
We couldn't keep him alive for you.
But all of us certainly tried."

"My loving child, you are forgiven.
I hope you will forgive me, too.
Although you did not hear me say it,
Please know that I've always loved you."

Pocketful of Forgiveness

You've got a pocketful of forgiveness.
Why don't you pass it around?
Or it could all turn to vengeance,
And begin to weigh you down.

Why are you still angry at your neighbor?
Why not just let him live?
You will find that if you reach out to him,
It will be easier for you to forgive.

You say a load is just a load,
But revenge can ruin your life.
Forgiveness is sure to lighten your load,
While vengeance keeps cutting like a knife.

His Cup Runneth Over with Revenge

He is almost filled with hatred
    and bitterness.
His mind is full of ways to
    get back at someone
    who has done him wrong.

There are no thoughts of forgiveness;
    no thoughts of mending the
    wall that would be
    strong enough to hold him up.

All ideas lead to ways to
    return the bad deeds
    which have come his way
    over the years.

He wants to pay back.
He wants to return the blows.
There is nowhere to store
    all of his anger.
His cup runneth over.

Yes, his cup runneth over with revenge.

Set Apart

Falling in Line with the World

*It's so much easier to fall in line
Than to stand up and try to do right.
It's easier to do what the world is doing
Than to hold my beliefs and fight.*

*I know I ought to set some standards
And be what God wants me to be.
I might even lose a friend sometimes,
But I'm just being me.*

*I know what God says about obedience.
I know the commitment I have to make.
Getting all mixed up in certain encounters
Is a chance I simply cannot take.*

*I can't fall in line with the entire world.
I want God to control my mind.
I want him to guide me in all I do.
I just cannot fall in line.*

No Reflection on You

You came to me and asked a favor.
It was something I could not do.
I felt I had to turn you down,
And it was no reflection on you.

Our lives are often filled with joy;
Again, there is so much pain.
Our sunny skies are clear and bright,
Until we see the clouds and rain.

We try to stay on the straight and narrow,
But there's a valley just below the peak.
And the time that we're most likely to fall
Is when our faith has become a little weak.

Uniqueness

Uniqueness seems to be one of my traits.
I'm unique in many places.
I want the world to see my uniqueness,
But not only by comparing faces.

Take a deeper look into my heart.
There is something inside to see.
The love I share with everyone
Is also a part of me.

Uniqueness is surely worth striving for;
It can help you hold your head up high,
When it seems that no one knows you're present
And the world is passing you by.

Uniqueness helps you say, "I forgive,"
Or to say an encouraging word,
To someone who is devastated
About something they may have heard.

Uniqueness makes you sing out praises,
When you've received something nice.
It makes you take the glory from yourself
And give it to Jesus Christ.

Let's go stretching for uniqueness.
Let's dare to be set apart.
People know how we look outside;
So let's introduce our hearts.

Be a Part of the Worship Service

Come out to worship expecting to give.
Then there's something you can get.
You shouldn't think that you will be entertained.
This is the sanctuary, not "the set."

There will be preaching and several hymns.
Come prepared to participate.
Don't mind if someone makes a profession of faith,
And we have to stay ten minutes late.

The choir can sing and so can you.
Neither has to be perfection.
If a couple of notes fly way off key,
Don't call the pastor about correction.

Give a part of yourself in the worship service.
Don't sit there and look so stern.
Find the scriptures printed in the bulletin.
There's a lot that you could learn.

Let the pastor deliver his message,
As God would have him present it.
See what words could improve your life,
Instead of finding ways to resent it.

Come out to worship and join right in.
Sing praises and honor the King.
You may not gain the entire world,
But you're not likely to lose one thing.

Sometimes

Sometimes I just want to do for others,
And let my own self be.
If I can help them along the way,
The Lord will take care of me.

Sometimes I'm filled with so much love,
There is simply no place to store.
The faster I distribute it,
The sooner I'm filled with more.

Sometimes I can't find one little thing,
That's wrong with this beautiful earth,
Until I think about a starving child,
Or one who died at birth.

Sometimes I look for a way to help.
I would do it at any cost.
And then I consider someone I know,
Still listed among the lost.

Sometimes I know it's not enough,
No matter how much I do.
So I keep on doing and asking for strength,
To start each day feeling new.

Sometimes this world seems only sweet,
And everything seems so bright,
Until I work at the shelter for homeless people,
Or see those sleeping on the streets at night.

Sometimes I feel there is happiness,
Enjoyed throughout the entire world.
But my happiness is dimmed with a parent's report
About a missing boy or girl.

Sometimes elderly people seem number one.
All are loved by families so dear.
So why are there so many days of loneliness,
With no one standing near?

Sometimes it appears this thing called freedom,
Is for people in every land,
Until I think about those in bondage,
Under the power of earthly hands.

Sometimes I wish these hopes of mine
Could be real in every heart,
With growing faith in a living God,
I will try to do my part.

A Slave to Sin No More

No more am I captured by
    the sins of this world
To the extent that I must
    fall into the hands of Satan
    whenever he wants me to fall.

I have a sense of peace and joy
    that would surely disgust him.
Because he knows
    I am working for a God
    who is too strong
To be challenged by a tiny force.

My way has been made clear now.
I must walk as though
I see the Light
    that comes only from above.
I must help others to see
    the goodness of His love.

Make Him Turn and Run

If you ever encounter the devil,
And he seems to get the best of you,
Listen to my scheme to get away.
Now here's what you have to do.

Just pretend that he is not around;
You never heard a word he said.
If he still tries to talk to you,
You don't even have to nod your head.

Let him know you're not his friend,
And his company you do not need.
If you let him think you like him,
More than likely he will succeed.

He'll always be standing by your side.
He will help you with every task.
He'll be with you doing everything,
And you won't even have to ask.

You'll try to conquer him from time to time.
You will tell him to go away.
He'll pretend that he doesn't hear you.
He will always find another way.

You've tried everything else; now try faith,
And watch as he starts to run.
Then you ought to wave good-bye to him.
Your new companion is the living Son.

Satan, I'm Going to Tell Jesus on You

Satan, I'm going to tell Jesus on you!
I'll report what you have done.
There is nothing you can do about it;
There is no need for you to run.

You had a chance to get away,
But you just kept on hanging around.
You've done bad deeds on everyone,
Wherever bad deeds could be found.

I'm telling Jesus on you, Satan!
I believe that you should know.
You thought you could get away free,
But now you see that is not so!

You won before, but not this time.
Your luck is running out!
You'd better get ready to settle down.
There will be no more moving about.

Peculiar People

Christians are peculiar people
Who walk a different way;
Who realize when there is a need,
And help others day by day.

Peculiar in a sense of love,
For those who are lonely and sad;
Peculiar in the way they live,
And try to make others glad.

Peculiar people are sometimes seen
As those of another time.
They do not keep up with sinful men,
And leave the Lord behind.

Christians are peculiar people.
They have a special mark.
Their light always shines brightly,
For those whose paths are dark.

If you don't mind being peculiar,
Let Jesus come into your heart.
He can make you become so different,
And now is the time to start.

Death

Believe on Him

How long can we hold on to our dream?
    How long to this limited life?
A better place is now prepared
    To end this growing strife.

Sickness comes and lingers a while.
    The struggle is so often great.
The final day has come at last.
    There is no longer wait.

God is Master, great and strong;
    His Power will sustain.
Trust Him with all your burdens:
    Believe on His precious name.

Fifty Years from Now

Fifty years from now, my friends,
I will probably be in my grave.
But if, by chance, I should still be here,
There are some thoughts I'd like to save.

I know I'll still be living for Christ,
And leading some others to Him.
If I should be able to teach His Word,
I will do it, but chances are slim.

I may be around in fifty years;
If so, this is how it will be.
I'll be encouragement for a lot of people,
For I will be over a hundred and three.

Preparing for the Inevitable

Getting old is inevitable,
But it is not as inevitable as death.
Getting old is something that
 may happen,
While death is something that
 will happen.

Her view of life is different
 from that of many folks.
There are some who won't talk
 about death.
They won't discuss their preferred
 resting place or their concern about
 eternity or their relationship with God.
They have no use for a burial plot.

But she wants to choose the place.
She wants to make the financial
 arrangements and spiritual contacts.
She wants to have something to say
 about the casket and the funeral.

If she lives to be an old woman,
She will at least be ready for
 the inevitable.

When Life Is Closing In

His life is closing in on him.
Sometimes he just can't make it.
If his life is not going to be meaningful,
Perhaps, the Lord will take it.

He has done a lot in his lifetime.
He could not have done much more.
He's glad that he can stand right there,
And greet people at the door.

Whenever you ask him how he's feeling,
He may just nod his head.
Quite often it's all that he can do,
To get himself out of bed.

But he's not giving up on this thing called life.
It's a battle one can't always win.
There are not many things left that he wants to do.
He feels that life is closing in.

We've Been Forgotten Day

It's going to be a grand celebration.
    You can't wait for Thanksgiving Day.
I wish we could feel the same as you,
    But we haven't been blessed that way.

Some of you will travel across your country,
    No matter what you have to pay.
My family and I will stay here starving,
    On this "We've Been Forgotten Day."

You'll have turkey with all the trimmings,
    With yams and fresh apple pie.
I'll watch my baby breathe her last few breaths.
    I just know she's going to die!

My baby has no water to drink.
    She is dying of hunger and thirst.
Her empty stomach is swollen so much,
    It looks like it's going to burst.

After you've had your Thanksgiving feast,
    Take a moment and look this way.
We'll still be starving and dying of thirst,
    On this "We've Been Forgotten Day."

Humor

Church Member Goes on Vacation

I'm not giving a tithe this month.
I think I'll leave a tip.
Too much money in the offering plate
Will ruin my summer trip.

I have to give a little something
Because the church is depending on me.
I just don't want to give too much;
So discretion here is the key.

The way I have this figured out,
I'll be back in a week or two.
I'll give a tithe in about a month,
And that's the best that I can do.

I know the bills will keep coming in,
And the church will have to pay.
The treasurer should be able to juggle the books.
I'm sure there is a way.

I'm not comfortable about doing this,
And what I'm doing doesn't sound too nice.
But since I cannot tithe this month,
A tip will just have to suffice.

Blame the Pastor

It's easy to blame the pastor,
When things are not going right.
He shouldn't have let it happen.
It was surely in his sight.

He should do more personal counseling,
When things are stirring up.
Meet with every member one-on-one,
Before the next communion cup.

He has got time to do it;
He's in his office all day long.
Sometimes he's there twelve hours a day.
He should correct whatever is wrong.

He has got all week to study,
And he should visit the young and old.
He should go to the hospital every day,
No matter whether it's hot or cold.

Every time the church door opens,
He should be sure that he is there.
If he cannot meet with every group,
That shows that he doesn't care.

He should also set a good example
By being with his children and wife.
He should be home with them every night,
To set a pattern for family life.

If there is a cleanup day on Saturday,
The pastor should grab a broom.
He should keep a paint brush in his hand,
Until they've painted every last room.

During the summer he should be present,
To keep Sunday School attendance high.
He'll be away when he goes to meetings,
Although most are held close by.

*He should not deprive his family
Of weekends at the sunny beach.
He should be there to show his love for them,
And he should stay here with us to preach.*

*The pastor may need to be two people.
Being one is not quite enough.
He has to be in too many places,
And he has to do too much stuff.*

*All these things have to be done.
Some of them the members must do.
There is no way that one body or mind
Can carry out the duties of a hundred and two.*

Surprise! Surprise! Surprise!

So you didn't go to church last Sunday?
    You went down to the lake,
And enjoyed the pleasures of the day,
    When you finally became awake.

You didn't tell the director;
    You didn't tell the pastor,
That you wouldn't be teaching your Bible class,
    Because you figured they could master.

Oh, let the members wonder where you are,
    Then come back as a big surprise.
Walk down the aisle a little bit late,
    As the people start to rise.

They don't need to know your business,
    Or when you will be away.
The class can find another teacher
    To take charge for just one day.

Perhaps the next time you'll stay a while,
  Like some of the others have done.
The surprise will really be more outstanding,
  If you miss more Sundays than one.

Don't worry about committee meetings,
  Or how the church will vote.
Don't tell the choir director you won't be there
  For that song with the highest note.

Sure, you practiced during the week;
  And wasn't that quite enough?
Doing the solo part on rehearsal night,
  Then again on Sunday, is tough.

Surprise everybody with your absence.
  Just be sure the pastor is there.
It doesn't matter if you don't show up;
  He is paid to do his share.

Demand prayer meeting on Wednesday night.
    You don't need to go.
It will be good for all the others,
    Who are sometimes feeling low.

Surprise the others on Sunday night,
    By the services unattended.
You didn't really want to have them;
    You merely recommended.

Now don't you give too much money,
    And surprise them by meeting your pledge.
Help keep the budget a little below,
    And keep the finance committee on edge.

Why support the special programs
    That compete with football games?
You went to Bible study last January.
    This one will be much the same.

But when it's time to join that Heavenly Team,
    And the players all start to rise,
The Heavenly Coach will leave you benched.
    Oh, Surprise! Surprise! Surprise!

Pointing Fingers at Them

Preacher, you really told them!
You really pointed out their sins.
You told those hypocrites about their faults,
And where the Christian life begins.

You really let them have it, Preacher!
You told them what they should have heard.
That'll teach them about fooling with you,
Because you really preach the Word.

They need to be here every Sunday,
So they can change their wicked ways.
Pretty soon they'll all be just like me—
Like me! Because they'll know it pays.

Some of them will learn a lesson.
Others will need a repeat.
They ought to be sitting where they can hear—
In the center, on a front-row seat!

You sure did tell them, Pastor!
And it really served them right.
That'll teach them about their deeds,
When they think they're out of your sight.

There are some who've been missing church,
And they were certainly not out of town.
Some of them were due up in the choir,
No matter how they may sound.

They're using "being gone" for a big excuse,
And I hope you'll get them straight.
While you're working on their conduct,
You can tell them about being late.

Oh, yes, you told them, Pastor!
Just like I knew you would.
It's about time they changed their ways,
And started doing something good.

The Pastor's Wife

They thought so much of the pastor's wife.
Some of them even tried to run her life.
Her daily attire couldn't be a mess,
So members wanted to tell her how to dress.

She couldn't buy anything from the discount store,
And she could not shop on the basement floor.
Neither could she buy from the classy boutique.
That was for people of fashion considered unique.

If she dressed too plainly, it would embarrass the crowd.
They criticized her for wearing colors too loud.
Expensive clothes meant the pastor earned too much,
An inexpensive wardrobe meant she was out of touch.

When she invited friends to come over and dine,
There was always jealousy on somebody's mind.
This social gathering took on a special twist,
Since no one at church had approved the guest list.

The pastor's wife had to be present for prayer,
Or members looked right at him and started to stare.
Many with children knew a mother's great task,
But if she didn't show up, they would always ask.

Being a pastor's wife is certainly no disgrace,
But members should try to let her take her place.
She should express her opinions the same as everyone else.
Most of all, she should be only herself.

Why can't everyone step back and just let her be.
Her imperfection, like ours, we all can see.
The most scrutinized member trying to live her own life
Is the person in church called the pastor's wife.

Invitations to Weddings and Funerals

*If you weren't invited to the wedding,
You shouldn't get mad and pout.
That's something very personal.
It's what decisions are all about.*

*The bride knows those she wants with her;
So may happiness always prevail.
Don't bring bad tidings on her wedding day.
Go ahead and wish her well.*

*Funerals and weddings have a lot in common.
There is not but one special honored guest.
If you are not the bride or in the casket,
Take your place with all the rest.*

*The groom is a very important person.
We can call him the V.I.P.
But when that bride starts down the aisle,
He seems as invisible as a man can be.*

*What if you should miss a funeral
Because the family wants it private and small?
That's no reason to get all puffed up.
The deceased is not complaining at all.*

*Your situation puts you with the living.
Please allow the dead to rest.
Instead of making such an effort to gripe,
Wish family members all the best.*

*Weddings and funerals are a lot alike;
They draw crowds from across the land.
They bring families together for the very first time,
Exchanging greetings and shaking hands.*

*People want to sit in special places
That will show the part they play,
Even those who have never done anything useful
Before the honored guest reached this day.*

*So you step back on these personal matters.
Attend if there's an invitation.
If not, you should continue with your daily life,
And stop the negative conversation.*

You're Sitting in My Seat

Good Morning! It's good to see you.
Is this your first time here?
I don't know why you're on this pew,
When so many other seats are near.

I know you are a visitor,
And your smile is wonderfully sweet.
But I simply must inform you
That you're sitting in my seat.

For the last twenty years I've been sitting here,
No matter what the occasion.
I would be pleased if you would move
Without any further Sunday persuasion.

There's an empty pew right behind you,
Or you may move across the aisle.
But I would appreciate your cooperation,
Because I've been sitting here for quite a while.

Thanks for moving and being so friendly.
I hope your visit will be an often repeat.
But if you should happen to come back again,
Please avoid sitting in my seat.

Get Me from the Church on Time

Why do we have to come to church
And sit here all day long?
We could have been finished and out of here,
If the choir hadn't done five songs.

I'm tired of all these announcements.
There are some I cannot remember.
The preacher is telling us every event
From January to the end of December.

It takes a real good breakfast
To nourish me through this long, long day.
We sit here in this hot churchhouse,
And sweat the Sabbath away.

There are too many different collections taken,
For every cause in the book.
The preacher's sermon is much too long;
There's a clock but he does not look.

Some of the congregation are paying attention.
There are people who are saying, "Amen!"
There are other members who are taking a nap,
While the preacher is shouting about sin.

He has been shouting for at least an hour.
Perspiration is forming a dome.
I wish he would let us out of here!
I'm hungry and I want to go home.

About the Author

Al Hall is an ordained deacon who served more than fifteen years as a Sunday School Director. Presently, he teaches a college and career young adult Sunday School class and is employed as the Equal Opportunity Program Manager with the USDA Forest Service in Washington, D.C. Al Hall received his bachelor's from Jackson State University and his master's from Western New Mexico University.

It's Trimmed in White If Color Makes Any Difference to You — the title comes from one of the poems in this collection — is Al Hall's second collection of poetry to be published. He is also the author of **There's Nothing Going Wrong With Your Head**. Al Hall resides in Alexandria, Virginia with his wife Lottie and their two sons, Tazh and Djawa.

To order **There's Nothing Going Wrong With Your Head**, send $13.00 to:
Al Hall
P.O. Box 11633
Alexandria, Virginia 22312-1906